D0045744

THE LANGUAGE OF
Flowers

CATHERINE LEE

THE LANGUAGE OF Flowers

RYLAND
PETERS
& SMALL

LONDON NEW YORK

*To my
flower fairy,
Emily Mary.*

SENIOR DESIGNER Megan Smith
SENIOR EDITOR Henrietta Heald
PICTURE RESEARCH Emily Westlake
PRODUCTION Eleanor Cant
ART DIRECTOR Anne-Marie Bulat
PUBLISHING DIRECTOR Alison Starling

Printed and bound in China.

First published in the USA in 2007
by Ryland Peters & Small, Inc.
519 Broadway
5th Floor
New York, NY 10012
www.rylandpeters.com

10 9 8 7 6 5 4 3 2 1
Text © Catherine Lee 2007
Design and photographs ©
Ryland Peters & Small 2007

Library of Congress CIP Data
Lee, Catherine.
 The language of flowers
   p. cm.
 Includes index.
  ISBN-10: 1-84597-282-1
  ISBN-13: 978-1-84597-282-0
 1. Flower language. 2. Symbolism of
flowers. 3. Flowers--Folklore. 4. Flowers--
Poetry. I. Title.
 GR780.L433 2007
 398'.368213--dc22
                    2006016083

Contents

THE ORIGINS OF THE
Language of Flowers

The custom of attributing meanings to flowers and plants can be traced back to ancient myths and fables from around the world, but the concept of a floral "language" is believed to have been introduced to Europe from Asia in the 18th century by the English writer Lady Mary Wortley Montagu and the French traveler Seigneur Aubry de la Mottraye. Letters written by Lady Mary on a visit to Turkey in 1717 mentioned the Persian "language of objects." The practice of associating objects with meanings also featured in de la Mottraye's account of his visit to the court of Charles XII in Turkey, published in 1727.

The idea of a language of flowers quickly became current in Europe. Charlotte de la Tour's *Le Langage des Fleurs*, a French dictionary containing more than 800 meanings for flowers, plants, and herbs, published in 1818, is thought to have been the basis of and inspiration for myriad books on the subject published internationally in subsequent years.

Assigning meaning to flowers grew immensely popular in Britain and North America during the Victorian era—perhaps because it allowed a freedom of expression otherwise frowned upon at the time. Feelings and emotions considered taboo could be expressed with flowers.

Given such a long history, it is not surprising that a definitive language of flowers doesn't exist. Several meanings can be linked to an individual flower or a single sentiment can be associated with more than one flower. It is the charm and romance of this tradition that makes saying it with flowers as desirable today as it has ever been.

Qualities & Virtues

Lost for words? Send a message of hope, comfort, support, or empathy in the form of flowers.

Anemone *Anemone*
* expectation

Aster, White *Aster*
* afterthought

Betony *Stachys officinalis*
* surprise

CHRYSANTHEMUM

Cyclamen *Cyclamen* * diffidence

Fuchsia *Fuchsia* * taste

Gentian *Gentiana* * integrity

CROWN IMPERIAL

Broom *Cytisus* * humility

Chervil *Anthriscus cerefolium* * sincerity

Chicory *Cichorium* * frugality

Chrysanthemum, White *Chrysanthemum* * truth

Cowslip *Primula veris* * pensiveness

Crown Imperial *Fritillaria imperialis* * power

ANEMONE

Goat's Rue *Galega* ∗ reason

Honesty *Lunaria* ∗ sincerity

Iris *Iris* ∗ a message

Magnolia *Magnolia* ∗ love of nature

Maple *Acer* ∗ reserve

Mimosa *Acacia* ∗ modesty

Mulberry, White *Morus* ∗ wisdom

Nasturtium *Tropaeolum* ∗ patriotism

Oleander *Nerium oleander* ∗ beware

PASSIONFLOWER

Sweet Briar *Rosa eglanteria*
* poetry

Sycamore *Acer pseudoplatanus*
* curiosity

Violet, Sweet *Viola*
* modesty

Olive *Olea europaea* * peace

Passionflower *Passiflora*
* belief

Planetree maple *Acer
pseudoplatanus* * curiosity

Primula *Primula*
* diffidence

11

DOUBLE DAISY

Artemisia *Artemisia*
* happiness

Crocus *Crocus* * cheerfulness

Crocus, Saffron *Crocus sativus*
* mirth

Double Daisy *Bellis perennis*
* enjoyment

CROCUS

Happiness

You don't need an excuse to give flowers to a friend or relative. An unexpected bouquet will bring instant joy and turn an ordinary day into something very special.

Gardenia *Gardenia* * ecstasy

Lesser Celandine *Ranunculus ficaria* * future joy

Lily of the Valley *Convallaria majalis* * return of happiness

London Pride *Saxifraga* x *urbium* * frivolity

Parsley *Petroselinum* * festivity

Ragged Robin *Lychnis flos-cuculi* * wit

Shamrock *Trifolium repens* * lightheartedness

Sweet Cicely *Myrrgus odorata* * gladness, mirth

Sweet Sultan *Amberboa moschata* * happiness

Sweet Vernal Grass *Anthoxanthum odoratum* * poor but happy

Tickseed *Coreopsis* * always cheerful

Tiger Lily *Lilium lancifolium* * gaiety

Violet, Yellow *Viola* * rural happiness

Wood Sorrel *Oxalis acetosella* * joy

13

Lily of the Valley

RETURN OF HAPPINESS

Give to me the happy mind,
That will ever seek and find
Something fair and something kind
All the wide world over.

ELIZA COOK (1818–89)

Happy the man, and happy he alone,

He, who can call to-day his own:

He who, secure within can say,

To-morrow do thy worst, for I have lived today.

JOHN DRYDEN (1631–1700)

Do you see O my brothers and sisters?

It is not chaos or death—it is form, union,

plan—it is eternal life—it is Happiness.

WALT WHITMAN (1819–92)

Friendship

Friendship is a gift to be treasured, and as we journey through life we learn to cherish old friends—as well as to delight in new ones. Express gratitude, admiration, or warm feelings for your friends by giving an extra-special gift of carefully chosen flowers.

Agrimony *Agrimonia eupatoria* ✳ thankfulness, gratitude

Amethyst violet *Browallia* ✳ admiration

Arborvitae *Thuja* ✳ unchanging friendship

SNOWDROP

Bellflower *Campanula* * gratitude

Boxwood *Buxus* * stoicism, constancy

Cactus *Mammilaria* * warmth

DAFFODIL

Canterbury Bells *Campanula medium* * constancy, gratitude

Chrysanthemum, Bronze *Chrysanthemum* * trust me

Coriander *Coriandrum sativum* * hidden worth

Daffodil *Narcissus* * regard

Dogwood, Flowering *Cornus florida* * durability

Geranium, Oak-leaved *Pelargonium quercifolium* * true friendship

Geranium, Scarlet *Pelargonium* * comfort

ZINNIA

Honesty *Lunaria* * honesty

Hyacinth *Hyacinthus*
* constancy

Mallow *Malva*
* good and kind

Oak *Quercus* * hospitality

Pear Tree *Pyrus communis*
* comfort

Peppermint *Mentha* x
piperita * warm feelings

Rhubarb *Rheum* x *cultorum*
* advice

Sage *Salvia* * esteem

Snowdrop *Galanthus*
* a friend in adversity

Spearmint *Mentha spicata*
* warm feelings

Star of Bethlehem
Ornithogalum * guidance

Zinnia *Zinnia*
* absent friends

STAR OF BETHLEHEM

Hyacinth CONSTANCY

Everyone calls himself a friend,
but only a fool relies on it;
nothing is commoner than the name,
nothing rarer than the thing.

JEAN DE LA FONTAINE (1621–95)

Our friends show us what we can do,
Our enemies teach us what we must not do.

JOHANN WOLFGANG VON GOETHE (1749–1832)

Better by far that you should forget and smile
Than you should remember and be sad.

CHRISTINA ROSSETTI (1830–94)

Fellowship is heaven, and lack of fellowship is hell;
fellowship is life, and lack of fellowship is death;
and the deeds that ye do upon the earth, it is for
fellowship's sake that ye do them.

WILLIAM MORRIS (1834–96)

Red roses are the flowers most commonly linked with expressions of love—but any one of a myriad other plants can also convey that special romantic sentiment.

Love & Passion

Arbutus, Trailing *Epigaea repens* ∗ rumors of love

Azalea *Rhododendron* ∗ romance

Bachelor's Buttons or Cornflower *Centaurea cyanus* ∗ delicacy

Beech *Fagus* ∗ lovers' tryst

SCABIOUS   PURPLE PANSY

Carnation *Dianthus*
* pure and deep love

Cedar *Cedrus*
* constancy in love

Chrysanthemum, Red
Chrysanthemum * in love

Columbine, Red *Aquilegia*
* anxious and trembling

Cranberry *Vaccinium
macrocarpon* * cure for
heartache

Cuckoo Flower *Cardamine
pratensis* * ardor

Dandelion *Taraxacum*
* lover's oracle

Daylily *Hemerocallis*
* coquetry

Dittany, White *Dictamnus
albus* * passion

Fern * fascination

Fuchsia *Fuchsia*
* humble love

Heliotrope *Heliotropium
arboescens* * infatuation,
adoration

Hollyhock *Alcea rosea*
* humble love

23

Hydrangea *Hydrangea*
* heartlessness

Impatiens *Impatiens*
* impatience

Jonquil *Narcissus jonquilla*
* desire

Lilac, Purple *Syringa* * first
emotions of love

LILAC

Lotus Flower *Nelumbo*
* estranged love

Mallow *Malva*
* consumed by love

Marigold, French *Tagetes
patula* * jealousy

Milkweed *Asclepias*
* heartache cure

HYDRANGEA

Motherwort *Leonurus cardiaca* ✳ secret love

Myrtle *Myrtus* ✳ love

Pansy, Purple *Viola* x *wittrockiana* ✳ you occupy my thoughts

Pincushion Flower *Scabiosa* ✳ unfortunate love

25

Rose LOVE

If love were what the rose is,
 And I were like the leaf,
Our lives would grow together
In sad or singing weather,
Blown fields or flowerful closes,
 Green pleasure or grey grief;
If love were what the rose is,
 And I were like the leaf.

A. C. SWINBURNE (1837–1909)

I ne'er was struck before that hour
With love so sudden and so sweet,
Her face it bloomed like a sweet flower
And stole my heart away complete.

JOHN CLARE (1793–1864)

All mankind love a lover.

RALPH WALDO EMERSON (1803–82)

All thoughts, all passions, all delights,
Whatever stirs this mortal frame,
All are but ministers of Love,
And feed his sacred flame.

SAMUEL TAYLOR COLERIDGE (1772–1834)

Shrimp Plant *Justicia* * perfect female loveliness

Spanish Jasmine *Jasminum grandiflorum* * sensuality

Rose *Rosa* * love

Rose, Blush *Rosa* * if you love me, you will find it out

Rose, Cabbage *Rosa* * ambassador of love

Rose, Full White *Rosa* * I am worthy of you

Rose, Red *Rosa* * I love you

Rose, Yellow *Rosa* * jealousy

Tuberose *Polyanthus tuberose* * dangerous pleasures

Tulip, Red *Tulipa* * declaration of love

Marriage

Flowers have long been associated with the wedding ceremony. During the years of marriage, giving flowers will bring back memories of that magical day.

CARNATION

30

DAHLIA

Black Bryony
Tamus communis
∗ be my support

Carnation *Dianthus*
∗ woman's love

Clover, White *Trifolium*
∗ I promise

Dahlia *Dahlia*
∗ forever thine

Geranium, Ivy *Pelargonium peltatum* ∗ bridal favor

Geranium, Oak-leaf
Pelargonium quercifolium
∗ true friendship

31

IVY

Hazel *Corylus*
* reconciliation

Holly *Ilex*
* domestic happiness

Honeysuckle *Lonicera* * fidelity,
the bond of love

Honeysuckle, Monthly *Lonicera*
* domestic happiness

Ivy *Hedera* * matrimony

Lavender *Lavandula*
* love and devotion

Lemon Blossom *Citrus limon*
* fidelity in love

Linden Tree *Tilia*
* matrimony

Oak Sprig *Quercus*
* hospitality

LAVENDER

Pansy *Viola* x *wittrockiana*
* you occupy my thoughts

Peony *Paeonia*
* happy marriage

Phlox *Phlox*
* united hearts

Plum Tree *Prunus domestica* * faithful until death

Rose, Bridal *Rosa*
* happy love

PANSY

Peony HAPPY MARRIAGE

He's more myself than I am. Whatever our
souls are made of, his and mine are the same.

EMILY BRONTË (1818–48)

34

'Twas when the spousal time of May
Hangs all the hedge with bridal wreaths,
And air's so sweet the bosom gay
Gives thanks for every breath it breathes.

COVENTRY PATMORE (1823–96)

Oh Happiness! our being's end and aim!
Good, pleasure, ease, content!
  Whate'er thy name:
That something still which prompts
  Th' eternal sigh,
For which we bear to love, or dare to die,
Which still so near us, yet beyond us lies,
O'er-look'd, seen double, by the fool, and wise.

ALEXANDER POPE (1688–1744)

35

Family

The unconditional love found in a family is unique, yet it is often taken for granted. Remind your relatives just what they mean to you with the gift of flowers.

Amaryllis *Amaryllis* * pride

Carnation *Dianthus* * woman's love

Convulvulus *Convolvulus* * bonds

Crown Imperial *Fritillaria imperialis* * pride of birth, power

Cuckoo Flower *Cardamine* * paternal error

Dittany of Crete *Origanum dictamnus* * birth

Heliotrope *Heliotropium arborescens* * devotion

AMARYLLIS

JUNIPER

Honeysuckle *Lonicera*
* the bond of love

Juniper *Juniperus*
* protection

Lilac *Syringa vulgaris*
* fraternal love.

Morning Glory *Ipomoea*
* affection

Moss * maternal love

Mountain Ash *Sorbus aucuparia* * I watch over you

CARNATION

Nettle *Urtica dioica* * unity

Oxalis *Oxalis*
* parental affection

Potentilla *Potentilla*
* beloved child, maternal affection

Primrose, Red *Primula vulgaris*
* unpatronized merit

Ranunculus *Ranunculus* *
memories of childhood

Sunflower, Dwarf *Helianthus*
* adoration

Verbena, Pink *Verbena*
* family union

Wood Sorrel *Oxalis acetosella*
* maternal tenderness

Beauty

Beauty, as they say, is in the eye of the beholder and manifests itself in many forms. What better way to tell someone that they are beautiful than with nature's embodiment of perfection—a flower?

Alyssum, Sweet *Lobularia*
* worth beyond beauty

Amaryllis *Amaryllis*
* splendid beauty

Cherry Blossom *Prunus*
* spiritual beauty

Common Camellia *Camellia japonica* * perfect beauty

Hibiscus *Hibiscus* * delicate beauty

Honeysuckle, French *Hedysarum coronarium* * rustic beauty

Hyacinth, White *Hyacinthus* * unobtrusive loveliness

Laburnum *Laburnum* * pensive beauty

Orchid *Orchis* * a belle

Ranunculus *Ranunculus* * radiant with charms

HIBISCUS

RANUNCULUS

Rose *Rosa* ✳ beauty

Rose, Damask *Rosa* ✳ brilliant complexion

Rose, Full-Blown *Rosa* ✳ you are beautiful

Rose, Moss *Rosa* ✳ voluptuousness

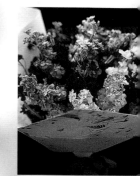

STOCK

ROSE

Stock *Matthiola*
* lasting beauty

Variegated Tulip *Tulipa*
* beautiful eyes

Venetian Mallow *Malva*
* delicate beauty

CHERRY BLOSSOM

Orchid
A BELLE

She was a phantom of delight

When first she beamed upon my sight.

WILLIAM WORDSWORTH (1770–1850)

For she was beautiful—her beauty made

The bright world dim, and everything beside

Seemed like the fleeting image of a shade.

PERCY BYSSHE SHELLEY (1792–1822)

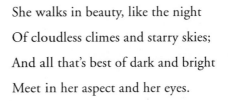

She walks in beauty, like the night
Of cloudless climes and starry skies;
And all that's best of dark and bright
Meet in her aspect and her eyes.

LORD BYRON (1788–1824)

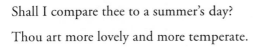

Shall I compare thee to a summer's day?
Thou art more lovely and more temperate.

WILLIAM SHAKESPEARE (1564–1616)

Buttercup *Ranunculus*
* childishness

Calla Lily *Zantedeschia*
* delicacy

Catchfly, Red *Silene*
* youthful love

CALLA LILY

Youth & Age

Celebrate the birthdays of your loved ones
with the beautiful gift of flowers. Glory in the
innocence and exuberance of youth and the
wisdom and contentment that comes with age.

Campion *Silene* ✳ youthful love

Centaury *Centaurium* ✳ felicity

Cherry Blossom *Prunus* ✳ spiritual beauty

Crocus, Spring *Crocus vernus* ✳ youthful gladness

Daisy *Bellis* ✳ innocence

European Cranberry Bush *Viburnum opulus* ✳ age

Fig *Ficus carica* ✳ longevity

Hyacinth *Hyacinthus* ✳ sport and play

Larkspur, Pink *Consolida* ✳ lightness

Lilac, White *Syringa* ✳ youth

Lily *Lilium* ✳ purity and modesty

Lily, White *Lilium* ✳ purity

Mallow *Malva* ✳ sweetness

47

Marjoram *Origanum*
* blushes

Meadow Saffron
Colchicum autumnale
* growing old

Medlar *Mespilus germanica*
* mature grace

ROSE BUD

CHERRY BLOSSOM   LILAC

Peony *Paeonia* ∗ diffidence and bashfulness

Poplar, White *Populus alba* ∗ time

Primrose *Primula vulgaris* ∗ early youth

Rosebud *Rosa* ∗ youth

Star of Bethlehem *Ornithogalum* ∗ purity

Wild Plum Tree *Prunus americana* ∗ independence

Willow *Salix* ∗ freedom

DAISY

Support your friends and family in their dreams and achievements. Send a bouquet of flowers for good luck or courage or to mark success.

Ambition & Success

Artemisia *Artemisia* ∗ good luck

Baby Blue Eyes *Nemophila* ∗ success everywhere

Buttercup *Ranunculus* ∗ riches

Cardinal Flower *Lobelia cardinalis* ✳ distinction

Cherry Laurel *Prunus lusitanica* ✳ perserverance

Chestnut Tree *Castanea* ✳ luxury

Columbine, Purple *Aquilegia* ✳ resolved to win

Coronilla *Coronilla* ✳ success to you

Daffodil *Narcissus* ✳ egotism

Foxglove *Digitalis* ✳ occupation, wish

Heather, White *Calluna* ✳ good luck

Hepatica *Hepatica* ✳ confidence

Hollyhock *Alcea* ✳ ambition

Lupine *Lupinus* ✳ imagination

Marsh marigold *Calha palustris* ✳ desire of riches

Orchid, Bee *Ophrys apifera* ✳ industry

DAFFODIL

BUTTERCUP

Osmunda *Osmunda*
* dreams

Palm *Palm* * victory

Polyanthus *Primula
polyantha* * confidence

Poplar, Black *Poplus nigra*
* courage, daring

Service Tree *Sorbus latifolia*
* prudence

Tulip *Tulipa* * fame

FOXGLOVE

SERVICE TREE

Success is counted sweetest
By those who ne'er succeed.
To comprehend a nectar
Requires sorest need.

EMILY DICKINSON (1830–86)

Tulip
FAME

Lowliness is young Ambition's ladder,
Whereto the climber upward turns his face.

WILLIAM SHAKESPEARE (1564–1616)

Even for learned men, love of fame
is the last thing to be given up.

TACITUS (AD c.56–AFTER 117)

I am a parcel of vain strivings tied
   By a chance bond together,
Dangling this way and that, their links
   Were made so loose and wide,
     Methinks,
    For milder weather.

HENRY DAVID THOREAU (1817–62)

Sadness & Loss

Many people find coping with loss profoundly difficult and it can be hard to know how to comfort them. When words fail, the gift of flowers can sometimes offer a little consolation.

Allspice *Calycanthus* * benevolence

Aloe *Aloe* * sorrow

Asphodel *Asphodelus aestivus* * regret

Bay *Laurus nobilis* * no change till death

Belladonna Lily *Amaryllis belladonna* * silence

Black Poplar *Populus nigra* * affliction

Butterfly Weed *Asclepias tuberosa* * let me go

Camellia *Camellia* * pity

Cedar *Cedrus* * think of me

SWEET PEA

Clover, White *Trifolium*
* think of me

Cypress *Cupressus* * despair,
death, mourning

Elecampane *Inula helenium*
* tears

Globe Amaranth *Gomphrena
globosa* * immortality

Harebell *Campanula
rotundifolia* * grief, pain

Helenium *Helenium* * tears

Hemp *Cannabis sativa* * fate

Hyacinth *Hyacinthus*
* benevolence

Hyacinth, Purple *Hyacinthus*
* sorrow

ROSEMARY   PINE

Jessamine, Carolina *Gelsemium
sempervirens* * separation

Lilac *Syringa* * memory

Locust *Robinia pseudoacacia*
* love beyond the grave

Michaelmas Daisy *Aster novi-
belgii* * farewell

Mimosa *Mimosa pudica*
* delicate feelings

Pansy, Purple *Viola* x
wittrockiana * you occupy
my thoughts

Pansy, Yellow *Viola* x *wittrockiana* * think of me

Pimpernel *Anagallis* * change

Pincushion Flower, Purple *Scabiosa* * unfortunate love

Pine, Austrian *Pinus nigra* * pity

Poppy *Papaver* * consolation

Poppy, White *Papaver* * sleep of the heart

Rose, Christmas *Helleborus niger* * relieve my anxiety

Rose, White *Rosa* * silence

POPPY

Rosemary *Rosmarinus officinalis* * remembrance

Snowdrop *Galanthus* * consolation

Sweet Briar *Rosa eglanteria* * sympathy

Sweet Pea *Lathyrus odoratus* * departure

Virgin's Bower *Clematis* * filial love

Wormwood *Artemisia absinthium* * absence

Sweet Pea DEPARTURE

'Tis better to have loved and lost
Than never to have loved at all.

ALFRED, LORD TENNYSON (1809–92)

Come to me in the silence of the night;

Come in the speaking silence of a dream;

Come with soft rounded cheeks and

    eyes as bright

As sunlight on a stream.

CHRISTINA ROSSETTI (1830–94)

Here are sweet peas, on tiptoe for a flight:

With wings of gentle flush o'er delicate white,

And taper fingers catching at all things,

To bind them all about with tiny rings.

JOHN KEATS (1795–1821)

INDEX

PICTURE CREDITS

Key: ph=photographer, a=above, b=below, r=right, l=left.

All photographs by Polly Wreford unless otherwise stated.

Page 2 ph Craig Fordham; 5 ph James Merrell; 6 ph Debi Treloar; 9b ph James Merrell; 10r ph Debi Treloar; 11l ph Pia Tryde; 12l ph Craig Fordham; 12r ph Francesca Yorke; 13 ph James Merrell; 13l ph Craig Fordham; 13ar ph Sandra Lane; 16l ph James Merrell; 18 ph James Merrell; 20 ph James Merrell; 21al ph Emma Lee; 23 ph Tom Leighton; 24b ph Craig Fordham; 28l & 28–29a ph Debi Treloar; 30 & 31al ph James Merrell; 32l ph Sandra Lane; 32r ph David Montgomery; 33 ph Sandra Lane; 34 main ph Dan Duchars; 35r ph David Brittain; 36 ph Alan Williams; 37 ph Debi Treloar; 39 ph Caroline Arber; 41a ph Jan Baldwin; 42 inset ph James Merrell; 45al ph David Brittain; 45br & 46br ph Craig Fordham; 48–49a ph James Merrell; 51 ph Henry Bourne; 52l ph Tom Leighton; 52r ph Melanie Eclaire; 53 ph Sandra Lane; 55r ph Pia Tryde; 57l ph Caroline Arber; 57r ph James Merrell; 58–59 ph Pia Tryde; 61al ph Debi Treloar; 64 ph Debi Treloar.